MW01489413

ISBN: 9798345415542

© 2024 Lise Pilot. All rights reserved.

No part of this publication may be reproduced, distributed, or transmitted in any form or by any means, including photocopying, recording, or other electronic or mechanical methods, without the prior written permission of the publisher, except in the case of brief quotations embodied in critical reviews and certain other noncommercial uses permitted by copyright law.

HOW TO LAND A JOB IN UX DESIGN

Your Guide to a Career in User Experience Design

TABLE OF CONTENTS

PREFACE

Recently, I posted a job opening at my company, hoping to assist anyone in my network to find design roles. To my surprise, that single post went viral, generating 10,000 impressions in a single week. Following this, I started receiving over 50 messages and connection requests a week.

My initial intention was to help every person who responded to my post. I replied and even chatted on the phone with connections who wanted career advice for a job in user experience design. As the messages piled up, I noticed a genuine hunger for information and a deep appreciation for my time.

Reflecting on my own journey as a UI/UX Designer for over two decades, I realized that I have a wealth of information to share. I think of how valuable it would have been to have a mentor like myself when I was younger. Someone who could equip me with the necessary skills and boost my confidence when applying to design jobs. Unfortunately, there weren't enough hours in the day to reply to every person with the information and guidance they deserved. Hence, I decided to compile the information into a book. If there's one piece of wisdom I have for those pursuing a career in high tech, it's this: it's not a straight line. Technology evolves rapidly, and companies must continuously adapt. This constant evolution leads to reorganization, restructuring, and reinvention to remain competitive. The single, most important quality for success is a positive, growth mindset.

My own career began after graduate school around 1995. I've witnessed two major technological advancements during my journey—the advent of the web and the rise of smartphones. Initially, we might not have realized we needed these innovations, but now we can't imagine life without them. Both of these events transformed the way people interact with the world around us.

The current transformational change, arguably even more significant, is the evolution of AI. While AI has existed for some time, recent advancements in computing power, the vast amount of global data, and the release of commercial AI products to the masses are driving exponential growth, making AI technology an integral part of our daily lives.

Each of these technological innovations has profoundly impacted how we work and how we live. They also present tremendous opportunities for careers in design because companies must learn to harness these innovations effectively in their products and services. As a user experience design professional, seizing these opportunities often depends on having a growth mindset and learning from every experience along the way.

When I was 18 years old, like many others, I didn't know what career path to pursue. Influenced by my parents, I chose the safe route and enrolled at the University of Massachusetts (UMass) to study Industrial Engineering. I was very much inspired by my father's career in engineering and business. His work involved optimizing product lines in manufacturing plants, saving them millions of dollars. He often brought home "goodies" from his business trips and shared stories. I vividly recall one occasion when he returned from a project at a candy factory, opening his briefcase to reveal fresh Reese's Cups straight from the production line. To this day, Reese's Cups are still my favorite candy,

During my junior year at UMass, I faced the decision of choosing a focus. When I met with my advisor to select classes, I expressed interest in Psychology and Ergonomic Design. Together, we created a customized degree path that incorporated Cognitive Psychology and Exercise Science. I graduated with a Bachelor of Science in Human Factors and Ergonomic Engineering.

During summer breaks, I interned as a Human Factors Engineer at Pitney Bowes. My responsibilities included usability testing for touch screen and speech recognition technologies used in mail tray processing systems. Additionally, I contributed to the industrial design of mail processing devices, such as handheld scanners and labeling equipment. I distinctly remember the experience of testing speech recognition accuracy in a lab environment, complete with ambient noise to simulate a mail processing facility.

After graduating from UMass, I attended Penn State University for my Master's in Industrial Engineering with a focus in Human Factors. During my second year, I accepted a one-year graduate student position at the IBM Human-Centered Computing Division in Boca Raton, Florida. In this role, I managed all apects of the Usability Lab, conducting tests on leading-edge speech recognition products.

My responsibilities included designing studies, recruiting participants from an agency, facilitating the studies, and synthesizing the results. This experience eventually led to a full-time position at IBM on the Human Factors Engineering team.

Around the year 1997, IBM closed its south Florida offices. Several executives opted for early retirement and went on to establish their own dot com startup companies. I received a confidential offer to become the Lead UX Designer for one of these startups. Intrigued, I left IBM and started an exciting journey in the South Florida high-tech startup circuit. Over the next few years, I encountered a mix of successes and challenges. One company went public, another was acquired, and yet another ran out of money. It was a rollercoaster and a great learning experience. I still have a paper stock certificate tucked away in my file cabinet along with my dream of receiving a quarter of a million dollars in an IPO payout. My father had a great piece of advice at the time... "If it sounds to good to be true, then it probably is".

After my ride with startups, I joined NTT/Verio as Sr. Usability Engineer in early 2001. In this position, I was responsible for running usability studies and improving the design of entrprise and consumer web hosting products. I experienced my first layoff in 2004 after having my first child. Undeterred, I decided to explore new op- portunities. That's when I applied to Citrix in Fort Lauderdale. I joined the Human Factors Design team at Citrix shortly after the team's formation. Little did I know that this would lead to a fulfilling ten-year role as a Lead UI/UX Product Designer.

As my career progressed, so did the team, and I grew alongside it. As Lead Product Designer, I managed all phases of UX Design for an enterprise product line that enabled employees to access virtualized apps and desktops from any device (we called it BYOD - "Bring Your Own Device"). It was a unique design challenge to secure corporate apps on employees' personal devices, as you can imagine.

The pinnacle of my career spanned from 2007 to 2012, during the emergence of capacitive touch smartphones and tablets. I still recall the moment when my manager told me, "I'm going to make you the Lead on iPhone." What? The iPhone had just hit the market and the app store was opening in just a few short months. This was a daunting task - designing for capacitive touch screen devices was brand new at the time, so not only did I have to figure out how to design for a completely new platform with a new mode of interaction (touch gestures), there were no published design guidelines or patterns. Having previously used a flip phone for several years, I found myself starting from scratch with no prior knowledge of smartphone design, but was energized by the challenge.

Over the next three years, I embarked on a journey to design our first-generation mobile app on six different mobile platforms: iOS, Android, WebOS, Windows Phone, Symbian, and Blackberry. Each vendor had multiple variations of their software operating system, catering to a diverse range of hardware form factors (with and without keyboards, trackpad/trackballs, stylus's, single gesture, mult-gesture...it goes on and on). Without physical devices in hand, I collaborated closely with the engineering team, relying on software emulators installed on virtual machines to design our apps until pre-release devices were available.

Our directive was clear: launch the first-generation app on "Day One" each app store opened. I championed the followoing approach...How might we ensure our apps would be identifiable as Citrix, yet appear designed for the native device - not just "installed on" the device? During this time, I established a virtualized mobile usability platform and designed a state-of-the-art usability lab, with special equipment for testing our mobile app prototypes on a range of smartphones and tablet devices.

After a rewarding decade at Citrix, I faced unexpected challenges in 2015 when the company experienced an extensive restructuring and layoffs. Despite my initial assumption of retiring with the company, the universe had other plans. Everyone should experience being laid off at some point in their career. It's a profound learning opportunity that fosters humility, resilience and growth.

I was not one who continually maintained a portfolio or continually kept my resume up to date. I had become lazy in external networking because I was instead managing internal company events such as Design Thinking workshops and helping organize employee cultural events such as Take Your Kids to Work day, so this blindsided me. I made the mistake of diving over confidently into job interviews, assuming I'd easily secure a position. But reality hit hard—without a flashy portfolio or carefully crafted online brand, it was difficult to showcase my worth. On top of that is the added challenge to put together a portfolio of samples while not showing anything proprietary and confidential.

For those of us not in Sales or Marketing, self-promotion doesn't come naturally. After a few ego-bruising experiences, I adopted the mindset to learn from each interview. Designing my personal "advertisement" became my priority. I tailored my resume and portfolio to align perfectly with the requirements of each position I pursued. In essence, it was a boot camp-style learning curve—fail fast, iterate, and refine until I landed a position. I even took interview opportunities purely for practice, regardless of whether I wanted to work for the company. Facing a room full of people, I knew the stakes were low if I stumbled.

The key takeaway? Embrace all experiences as learning opportunities, whether positive or negative. Shift your mindset: there are no "bad" experiences—only chances to learn and grow. Stepping out of your comfort zone is essential. Supporting my family with two young children and unable to relocate easily—was my driving force to look for opportunities where none seemed apparent.

Opportunities often emerge from unexpected sources. My next position came about during a casual conversation with another parent at my son's baseball game. As we sat in the stands, I worked on my portfolio on my laptop, which sparked a discussion. This parent had recently met someone in an airport lounge—an individual in the process of forming a high-tech startup company in Fort Lauderdale. He graciously shared the contact information, and I took the initiative to cold-call the company's founding owner.

To my surprise, they hadn't realized their need for a UX Designer to design their products and services, despite having already hired several software engineers. I eagerly invited myself to their office, and passionately pitched why they needed a UX Designer and how my expertise could benefit them. The result? They created a UX Architect position specifically for me.

Over the next year and a half, I assembled a small UX Design team and established a user-centered design process for this company. Applying a client-centered approach, my efforts yielded products that exceeded customer expectations. We celebrated our achievements with a successful world premiere grand opening, showcasing demos of RFID track-and-trace solutions for retail, hospitals, and grocery stores in our state-of-the-art technology showroom. It was an exciting adventure.

Here's the catch: when I created the position at the startup company, they couldn't offer me competitive compensation, and I actually took a salary decrease. However, I saw it as an opportunity to learn new technologies (IoT, Blockchain, RFID tracking) and refresh my UI/UX Design portfolio. I treated each project as a portfolio case study, often arriving early or staying late to meticulously document every phase of my design process. You see, despite not landing the exact position I desired, I gained substantial value from that role.

In 2016, I had past colleagues working at another high-tech company in the area—Ultimate Software. It felt like a perfect fit. Encouraged by my peers, I interviewed with a fresh portfolio showcasing recent samples from my time at the startup company. The interview process was extensive, but eventually, I secured a position as Lead User Experience Designer. I quickly advanced to managing a team of designers and researchers for a key product line. I now hold the role of Principal UI/UX Designer, leading design initiatives for enterprise software features utilizing the latest, leading-edge technologies.

Career Timeline

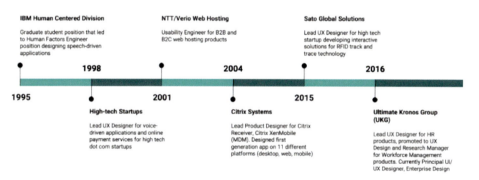

My two decades' long career in this field has yielded countless stories and valuable lessons. While this summary provides a glimpse into my journey, remember that this book was written for anyone just starting out or looking to advance their career in UX Design. Thank you for your interest and passion, and I hope you find this book a good stepping stone on your path.

Be sure to drop me a note on LinkedIn!

PART 1. Intro to User Experience (UX) Design

01 What is User Experience Design?

Have you ever used an app so intuitive it felt like it read your mind? Or browsed a website so beautifully designed that using it was a pleasure in itself? If so, you've experienced the power of good design. But what exactly is UX design? UX stands for User Experience. UX design is the process of designing products and experiences that are not only functional but engaging and enjoyable.

A UX designer acts as an advocate for the user throughout the design process. Their primary focus is on understanding user needs, behaviors, and motivations. By conducting user research and employing empathy, UX designers can create products that are:

- **Useful:** Fulfills a user's needs and helps them achieve their goals.
- **Usable:** Easy to learn, navigate, and use, regardless of technical expertise.
- **Desirable:** Appealing to the user aesthetically and emotionally, creating a positive experience.
- **Accessible:** Inclusive and usable by people with disabilities.
- **Engaging:** Motivates users to continue interacting in a positive way.

The field of UX design is booming, with an ever-increasing demand for skilled professionals.

User Experience

Key Components

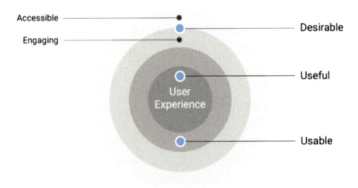

User Experience design principles apply across a variety of products and digital experiences from the very first touch point to the last.

- **Mobile Apps:** From banking apps to social media platforms, UX design ensures a smooth and intuitive experience on connected devices.
- **Websites:** Clear navigation, well-organized information, and visually appealing layouts are all hallmarks of good website design.
- **Software Applications:** UX design helps users navigate complex software programs efficiently and find the features they need quickly.
- **Physical Products**: Even physical products benefit from UX design considerations, focusing on usability, ergonomics, and user interaction with the product.

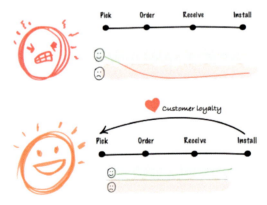

THE IMPACT OF UX DESIGN

UX design has a profound impact on the success of business. Here's how:

√ **Increased Customer Satisfaction:** Good UX design leads to happy and satisfied users. People who find a product easy and enjoyable to use are more likely to keep using it and recommend it to others.

√ **Improved Business Performance:** Satisfied users translate to increased customer loyalty, brand reputation, and ultimately, higher revenue.

√ **Reduced Development Costs:** Identifying usability issues early in the design process through UX research can save time and money compared to fixing problems after a product launch.

√ **Reduced Support Costs:** Getting it right the first time can potentially save millions of dollars annually in its cost to serve.

√ **Enhanced Brand Loyalty:** A well-designed product reflects positively on the brand, creating a perception of innovation, user-centricity, and overall quality.

Customer Experience (CX) Pyramid

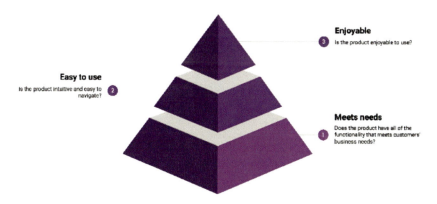

Enjoyable
3 Is the product enjoyable to use?

Easy to use
Is the product intuitive and easy to navigate? 2

Meets needs
Does the product have all of the functionality that meets customers' business needs? 1

THE ROLE OF A UX DESIGNER

User Experience (UX) Designers play a crucial role in creating products that are not only efficient and accessible but also enjoyable to use. Here's a detailed look at what a User Experience Design Professional does:

1. **User Research:** Conducts research to understand the needs, behaviors, and motivations of people. This may involve interviews, observations, surveys, and usability tests to gather data that informs design decisions.
2. **User Personas and Scenarios:** Creates detailed profiles of target users and scenarios to simulate real-life use cases. These personas help ensure the product design aligns with user expectations and needs.
3. **Wireframes and Prototypes:** Creates basic outlines (wireframes) and more detailed interactive models (prototypes) of products. These tools are used to visualize and test design concepts.
4. **User Testing:** Organizes testing sessions to collect feedback from users. This feedback is critical to iterating and improving the product.
5. **Collaboration with Stakeholders:** Works closely with Product Managers, engineers, and other stakeholders to ensure designs are feasible and align with business goals and technical constraints.
6. **Interaction and Visual Design:** Designs the ways people interact with a product or service, including the aesthetics like layout, colors, fonts, and images, to create a cohesive and pleasant experience.
7. **Accessibility and Inclusivity:** Ensures the product is accessible and usable for as many people as possible, including those with disabilities. This includes designing user interfaces that work well with accessibility features on all platforms.
8. **User Feedback Monitoring:** Continuously improves the customer experience based on channels of customer feedback and market sentiment.
9. **Documentation and Delivery:** Creates specification documents that serve as a blueprint that software developers and stakeholders can use to build and deliver the product or service.

In essence, a UX Designer's job is to bridge the gap between the user, the technology, and the business, ensuring that the product not only meets peoples' needs but also functions well and creates an enjoyable experience for all users.

02 The UX Design Process

The magic of UX design doesn't happen overnight. It's a structured, iterative process that involves understanding user needs, translating needs into concepts, and testing and refining alternative solutions. This chapter will walk you through the stages of a UX design project from understanding peoples' needs to creating the products and services they love.

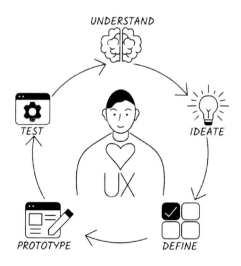

1. EMPATHIZE: USER RESEARCH

The foundation of good UX design lies in understanding the users. This initial stage involves gathering information about the target audience through various user research methods:

- **User Interviews:** In-depth conversations with users to uncover their needs, pain points, goals, and mental models.
- **Surveys and Questionnaires:** Quantitative research methods to gather data from a broader user base, gauging user sentiment and preferences.
- **Customer Community:** A valuable Voice of the Customer (VoC) channel where customers share real world anecdotal information and workarounds to solve common problems they are experiencing.
- **Sales, Services and Support:** An often overlooked asset, designers should explore the feedback customer-facing stakeholders receive from clients. This is particularly important for uncovering the root causes of the most expensive support cases.
- **User Persona Development:** After gathering everything you know about the users, research data can be synthesized into user archetypes that represent different user roles with specific goals, needs and behaviors.

2. DEFINE: DEFINE THE PROBLEM AND SCOPE

Based on user research findings, the design team defines the core problem the product aims to solve and outlines the project scope. This stage involves:

- **Problem Statement Formulation:** Clearly articulating the specific problem the product will address for the target users.
- **User Needs and Goals Identification:** Defining the key needs and goals users are trying to achieve when using the product.
- **Product Vision and Functionality Determination:** Establishing the overall vision for the product and the core functionalities it will offer.
- **Prioritization and Feature Creep Avoidance:** Focusing on the most critical features that address user needs while avoiding feature creep, the tendency to overload the product with unnecessary functionalities.

3. IDEATE: BRAINSTORMING AND CREATIVE EXPLORATION

With a clear understanding of the problem and user needs, the team enters the creative exploration phase. This stage involves:

- **Brainstorming Sessions:** Generating a wide range of ideas for potential solutions through collaborative workshopping sessions.
- **Information Architecture (IA) Development:** Structuring content and functionalities in a logical and user-friendly way, ensuring users can easily find what they need.
- **User Flow Creation:** Mapping out the steps users will take to achieve their goals within the product, ensuring a smooth and efficient user journey.

4. PROTOTYPE: BUILDING INTERACTIVE MOCKUPS

This stage focuses on creating prototypes, which are basic models of the product's interface and functionality. Prototypes range in level of fidelity - from low fidelity paper prototypes to higher fidelity digital prototypes. When considering the detail of your prototype, it's important to adjust your fidelity to the type of feedback desired. For example, you don't want to show something very polished and realistic when you want to your participants to focus on the flow of tasks and not the graphical treatment. It's important to start scrappy so participants don't think you've invested too much time and would be tentative to provide candid feedback.

- **Low-fidelity prototypes:** Hand-sketched on paper or black and white using digital wireframing tools. Focus on conveying core user flows and interaction patterns, not visual aestheics.
- **Medium-fidelity prototypes:** Click through prototypes created from wireframes that are limited in functionality and typically just stringed together using basic hotspots.
- **High-fidelity prototypes:** Only useful in the later stages of design after several iterations have already been vetted and revised with users. Highly interactive to mimic the real product, with close to final graphical treatment and branding. Can be used to socialize specifications when handing off designs to developers.

5. TEST: USER FEEDBACK AND ITERATION

The prototypes are then put to the test with real users. Usability testing allows the team to identify any usability issues and areas for improvement to ensure the design aligns with user expectations. Based on user feedback, the design team iterates on the prototype, refining the interface and functionalities until he ideal product experience is achieved.

- **Participant Recruiting:** Participants in the study should possess a background and experience similar to that of the target users for your product or service.
- **Number of Participants:** Typically, having 4-6 participants per test iteration is adequate for identifying common usability issues.
- **Observation:** Having project stakeholders observe the sessions or review the recorded sessions is highly beneficial. This allows team members to witness real people interacting with the prototype. I prefer conducting a debrief session with my project team after each session to reach a consensus on our observations and determine areas for improvement in subsequent iterations based on the feedback received.

6. REFINE: DESIGN ITERATION AND DEVELOPMENT

Following user testing, the design team iterates on the prototypes, incorporating user feedback and refining the visual design based on guiding design principles.

- **Iterative Testing and Refinement:** Perform iterative testing and designs until user feedback indicates it's the right solution.
- **Brand Style Guide:** Stylize the product's visual language, including typography, colors, and UI elements, ensuring consistency throughout the design and adherence the company's brand.
- **Technical Feasibility:** Review designs with engineering architects to ensure the experience you are proposing can be implemented with the company's current technology.
- **Accessibility (A11y):** Review designs for adherence to accessbility guidelines and specify details that will make your product work well with accessbility technologies such as screen readers.

Design Process

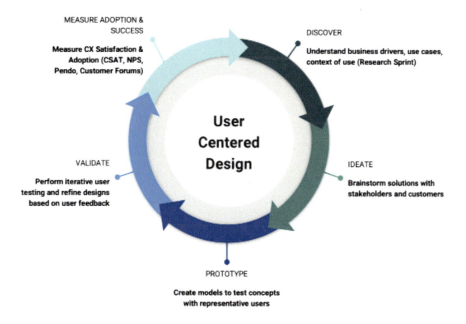

7. MEASURE: FEEDBACK AND MONITORING

The design process doesn't end with launch. Once the product is released, it's crucial to measure success and adoption through analytics tools and user reviews. This ongoing feedback loop allows the design team to identify areas for improvement and iterate on the product to maintain a positive user experience.

- **Google Analytics or Pendo:** Analytics tools can measure the number times or amount of time users engage with a feature, and the path they take through the product experience to achieve a goal.
- **Customer Community:** Customers can post questions, feedback or reviews in a public forum that can be monitored for ideas on improvements.
- **Sales & Services:** Internal stakeholders can report on feedback they get from customers in the field, which can inform future product roadmaps.

Each metric provides unique insights, collectively offering a comprehensive view of the user experience.

The following graphic presents a hierarchy of key metrics to assess user satisfaction and experience:

:

- **Goal Completion Rate (GCR):** Measures if users achieve their objectives using the product, answering the question, "Did it meet their needs?"
- **Customer Effort Score (CES):** Evaluates how easy it is for users to complete tasks, answering the question, "Was it easy to use?"
- **Customer Satisfaction Survey (CSAT):** Captures overall enjoyment and satisfaction from the interaction, answering the question, "How was the experience?"
- **Net Promoter Score (NPS):** Gauges the likelihood of users recommending the product to others, answering the question, "How likely will you be to recommend the product to others?"

03 The Research Sprint

A Research Sprint is a focused, time-bound process designed to quickly gather insights about users, their needs, and behaviors to inform product development and design. Similar to a Design Sprint, which focuses on rapidly prototyping and testing solutions, a Research Sprint emphasizes the initial phases of understanding user needs and validating assumptions through concentrated research efforts. Here's what typically happens in a Research Sprint.

OBJECTIVES OF RESEARCH

Typically lasting from a few days to a week, Research Sprints are short to ensure fast results and maintain focus on specific research goals.

The primary goal is to gain deep insights into user behaviors, needs, and challenges that inform and inspire the design process. It often involves identifying opportunities for innovation or areas needing improvement in existing processes.

KEY PHASES OF RESEARCH

1. **Planning and Preparation**
   - **Define Objectives:** Clearly articulating what you need to learn from the research to make informed decisions.
   - **Recruit Participants:** Identifying and recruiting suitable participants who represent the target user base.
2. **Conducting Research**
   - **Method Selection:** Choosing appropriate research methods based on objectives. Common methods include interviews, ethnographic field studies, usability testing, and surveys.
   - **Data Collection:** Gathering data through selected methods within the set time frame.
3. **Analysis and Synthesis**
   - **Data Analysis:** Reviewing and analyzing the data collected to draw meaningful insights.
   - **Insight Generation:** Synthesizing findings into actionable insights that can inform product features, user flows, or overall strategy.
4. **Reporting and Recommendations**
   - **Stakeholder Presentation:** Presenting findings and recommendations to stakeholders to inform decision-making.
   - **Documentation:** Documenting the process and outcomes in a format that is useful for ongoing and future projects.

OUTCOMES OF RESEARCH

A Research Sprint in User Experience Design yields invaluable insights that lay the foundation for informed and user-centric design decisions. The outcomes of this intensive research phase often include a wealth of qualitative and quantitative data that illuminate user behaviors, preferences, and pain points.

Key artifacts produced during this sprint are pivotal in translating research findings into actionable design strategies.

- **Personas:** Detailed, semi-fictional representations of target users that encapsulate their demographics, motivations, goals, and challenges.
- **Journey Maps:** Visualizations of the user's end-to-end experience with a product or service, highlighting key touchpoints, emotions, and potential areas for improvement.

These tools enable the design team to empathize with users and identify opportunities for innovation and enhancement, thereby setting the stage for a successful Design Sprint.

Customer Journey

04 The Design Sprint

A Design Sprint is a time-constrained, structured process used to rapidly ideate, prototype, and test concepts with users. Originally developed by Google Ventures, it's designed to improve the chances of making something people will actually want, in a fraction of the time it would traditionally take. The sprint helps teams to clearly define goals, validate assumptions, and create a roadmap for successful products or features.

DESIGN SPRINT WORKSHOP

The traditional Design Sprint workshop involves 8-12 stakeholders from various disciplines working together. It's beneficial to include representatives from Product Management, Engineering, Design, Sales, Support, and any other departments that can provide valuable insights.

1. **Day 1: Understand and Define** - On the first day, the team focuses on understanding the problem space. This involves sharing knowledge, understanding user needs, and defining the scope of the challenge. The day ends with setting a clear goal for the sprint and a specific target for the prototype to be tested.

2. **Day 2: Diverge and Decide** - The second day is all about generating a broad range of ideas and solutions. Team members independently sketch different approaches to solve the problem, following which the team collaboratively reviews these sketches. The day concludes with decision-making processes, like dot voting or critique sessions, to select the most promising ideas.

3. **Day 3: Prototype** - On this day, the focus is on turning the selected ideas into a prototype that is realistic enough to test with users. The aim is to create models of the product ideas without the need for fully functional development.
4. **Day 4: Test** - The fourth day is dedicated to testing the prototype with real users. Typically, five users are enough to uncover any major issues. The team observes how users interact with the prototype and gathers feedback on its effectiveness and usability.
5. **Day 5: Learn and Iterate** - The final day involves processing the feedback from user tests, learning about the strengths and weaknesses of the concept, and deciding on the next steps. These might include iterating on the prototype, starting a new sprint to explore other aspects of the problem, or moving forward with development based on the validated concepts.

Design Sprints are highly effective in helping teams to move quickly from ideas to validated solutions, making them popular among startups and large organizations alike. They're particularly useful when there's a need to break through stalemates in development or when tackling complex problems that need rapid innovation.

A MODIFIED DESIGN SPRINT APPROACH

In a modified approach, the user research is completed and synthesized before the workshop, and the protyping and testing can be done in the days and weeks after the workshop. Designers and stakeholders like this approach because it enables more time for collaborative idea generation and sketching while everyone is together.

Pre-Workshop ("Research Sprint")
- **Research and Interviews:** Conduct thorough user and market research to gather insights and prepare detailed findings at the start of the workshop.
- **Scope Definition:** Clearly define what's in scope, out of scope, and the nice-to-haves for the sprint.

2. **Sprint Worshop**
    - **Day 1 - Understand:** Review research findings and define the long-term goals. Participants write down 'How Might We' (HMW) questions to explore potential solutions.
    - **Day 2 - Collaborate:** Discuss the perfect and problematic future scenarios and develop a user story map to visualize the future flow.
    - **Day 3 - Sketch:** Individuals sketch their ideas, inspired by research insights and competitive reviews.
    - **Day 4 - Vote and Combined Sketch:** Team members pitch their designs, followed by a silent voting session to select the best ideas, which are then combined into a final concept.
3. **Post-Workshop Story Breakdown:** The business analyst (BA) collaborates with developers and engineers to categorize and prioritize work.
    - **Prototype Building:** The UX Designer develops a prototype based on the team-agreed concept, suitable for user testing.
    - **Customer Validation:** The UX Designer or Researcher conducts user testing with the prototype.
    - **Iteration and Detailed Design:** Feedback from user testing is used to refine designs until the best solution is accepted by users.
    - **Internal Reviews:** The UX Design Lead brings the designs to the Brand, Accessibility and Design Language System (DLS) teams to ensure the designs comply with the company's established design standards.

Design Sprint Timeline

Design Sprint Timeline

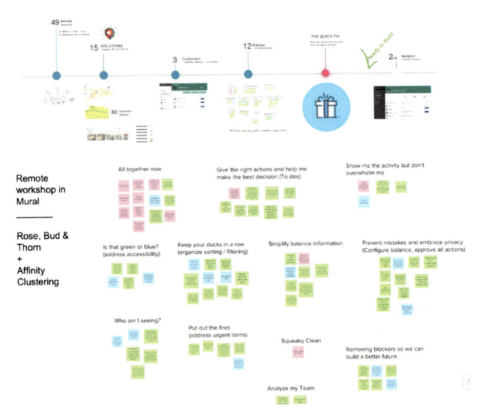

Remote workshop in Mural
_____
Rose, Bud & Thorn
+
Affinity Clustering

All together now

Give the right actions and help me make the best decision (To dos)

Show me the activity but don't overwhelm me

Is that green or blue? (address accessibility)

Keep your ducks in a row (organize sorting / filtering)

Simplify balance information

Prevent mistakes and embrace privacy (Configure balance, approve all actions)

Who am I seeing?

Put out the fires (address urgent items)

Squeaky Clean

Removing blockers so we can build a better future

Analyze my Team

Sketching and Voting

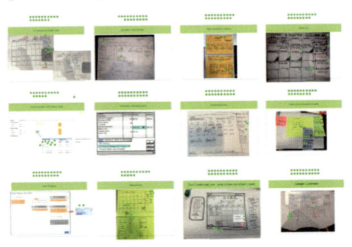

REMOTE PARTICIPATION

Ideally, all team members should be physically present in the room. However, it is increasingly common to have members participate remotely in design sprint workshops. Remote participants are not limited to virtual employees; local team members may also need to join remotely if they cannot come to the office that day. Therefore, it's best to always be prepared.

Preparation for Remote Participants:

- Set up a virtual meeting using tools like Google Meet, Webex, etc. This should also serve as your chat channel for communication.
- Set up a virtual whiteboard tool such as Mural, Freehand, or FigJam.
- Include all virtual meeting and whiteboard links in the invitation.
- Connect webcam to show participants in the room, and encourage remote participants to have their webcam on to maximize engagement.
- Arrive early to set up audio and cameras to ensure your workshop starts on time.

Remote Workshop Mural Board

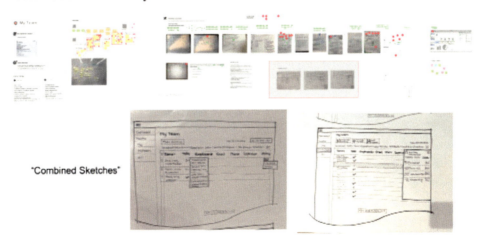

"Combined Sketches"

05 User Flows, Wireframes & Prototypes

The designing phase is crucial for transforming insights into actionable designs. By meticulously crafting user flows, wireframes, and prototypes, UX designers can create intuitive and user-friendly interfaces that meet user needs and business objectives. Testing these prototypes with representative users provides invaluable feedback, ensuring the final product delivers a seamless and satisfying user experience.

USER FLOWS

User flows are diagrams that map out the steps a user takes to complete a specific task within an application or website. They help visualize the path users will take and highlight the various interactions they will encounter.

Steps to Create User Flows:

1. **Identify User Goals:** Begin by understanding what the user wants to achieve. This could be anything from purchasing a product to signing up for a newsletter.
2. **Define Key Tasks:** Break down the user goals into smaller tasks that need to be completed. Each task should represent a step in the user journey.
3. **Map the Flow:** Use flowchart symbols to represent different screens, decisions, and actions. Arrows indicate the direction of user movement through the application.

4. **Review and Refine:** Collaborate with stakeholders and team members to review the flow. Make adjustments based on feedback to ensure the flow is logical and efficient.

Example: Consider a user flow for an e-commerce checkout process. It would include steps such as browsing products, adding items to the cart, entering shipping information, selecting a payment method, and confirming the purchase.

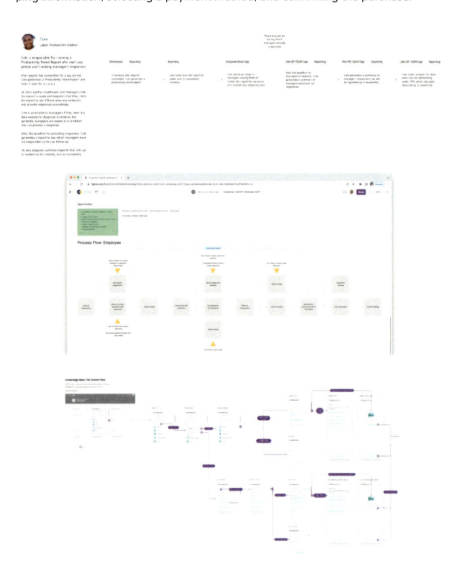

WIREFRAMES

Wireframes are low-fidelity representations of a web page or app screen. They focus on layout, structure, and content placement without aesthetic details such as color schemes or typography.

Steps to Create Wireframes:
1. **Sketch Basic Layouts:** Start with rough sketches on paper or a whiteboard.
2. **Use Wireframing Tools:** Tools like Sketch, Figma, or Adobe XD allow you to create digital wireframes. These tools offer pre-built UI components that can be dragged and dropped into place.
3. **Define Content Hierarchy:** Prioritize content based on user needs and business goals. Ensure that important elements are prominently displayed and easily accessible.
4. **Add Annotations:** Include notes to explain interactions, such as button functions, link destinations, and input fields. This helps developers and stakeholders understand the intended functionality.
5. **Review and Iterate:** Share wireframes with the team for feedback. Iterate on the design based on suggestions and insights to improve usability and clarity.

Example: A wireframe for a product detail page might include a product image, title, price, description, "Add to Cart" button, and related products section.

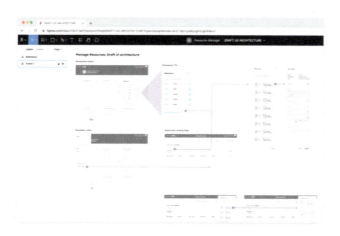

PROTOTYPES

Prototypes are interactive models of a web page or app that simulate the user experience. They are used for usability testing to gather feedback from representative users.

Steps to Create Prototypes:
1. **Choose the Right Fidelity:** Decide on the fidelity of your prototype. Low-fidelity prototypes are simple and quick to create, while high-fidelity prototypes closely resemble the final product. It's always best practice to start "scrappy" so user testing participants focus on flow and content, and aren't influenced by how polished it looks.
2. **Build Interactive Elements:** Use prototyping tools like InVision, Sketch, Figma, or Axure RP to create clickable elements and transitions. These tools allow you to simulate user interactions, such as clicking buttons or navigating between screens.
3. **Test Scenarios:** Develop scenarios for testing, ensuring they cover the key tasks identified in the user flows. Scenarios should be realistic and representative of actual user behavior.
4. **Conduct Usability Testing:** Recruit representative users to test the prototype. Observe their interactions, ask questions, and gather feedback on usability and overall experience.
5. **Analyze Feedback and Iterate:** Analyze the feedback to identify pain points and areas for improvement. Iterate on the prototype, making necessary adjustments to enhance the user experience.

Example: A high-fidelity prototype of an e-commerce checkout process would allow users to click through each step, from adding products to the cart to entering payment information and completing the purchase.

06 Design Principles

As you embark on your journey to become a UX designer, understanding the foundational principles that guide design decisions within organizations is crucial. Guiding design principles are a set of core values and standards that dictate how products should be designed and developed within an organization. They reflect a company's vision, goals, and the needs of their users. These principles are not just abstract concepts; they are practical, actionable guidelines that help designers make decisions that align with the organization's objectives and user expectations.

COMMON DESIGN PRINCIPLES

While each company may have its unique set of principles, there are common themes that many organizations embrace:

1. **Simplicity:** Design should be understandable and straightforward, minimizing user effort to learn and use a product.
2. **Consistency:** Ensuring a uniform experience across all touchpoints enhances user trust and reduces confusion.
3. **Accessibility:** Products should be usable by people of all abilities and disabilities, emphasizing inclusivity.
4. **Usability:** Products must be functional and practical, solving real problems for users efficiently.
5. **Engagement:** Design should captivate and hold the user's attention, providing delightful experiences.

THE VALUE OF DESIGN PRINCIPLES

When faced with design decisions, principles provide a clear framework for making choices that align with the company's goals. This can speed up the design process by reducing ambiguity.

- **Alignment and Cohesion:** Guiding principles ensure that everyone in the organization—from designers to developers to marketing teams—is on the same page regarding what good design means for the company. This alignment is crucial for maintaining a coherent brand identity and user experience across products and services.
- **Quality and Consistency:** These principles act as a quality control measure, ensuring that all design outputs meet a certain standard and are consistent, which is vital for brand recognition and user satisfaction.
- **Efficiency in Decision Making:** When faced with design decisions, principles provide a clear framework for making choices that align with the company's goals. This can speed up the design process by reducing ambiguity.
- **Innovation and Creativity:** These principles act as a quality control measure, ensuring that all design outputs meet a certain standard and are consistent, which is vital for brand recognition and user satisfaction.

IMPLEMENTING GUIDING DESIGN PRINCIPLES

As a UX designer, whether you are working within a large company or a startup, understanding and applying these principles is part of your job. Here's how you can effectively implement them:

1. **Learn and Internalize:** When you join a company, take time to thoroughly understand its guiding design principles. These are often found in design manuals or onboarding materials.
2. **Apply Them in Your Work:** Use these principles as a checklist against every design decision you make. Whether you are wireframing, prototyping, or testing, ask yourself if your designs align with the principles.
3. **Advocate and Educate:** As you grow in your role, help propagate these principles within your team and beyond, especially if you notice gaps in their application.
4. **Review and Adapt:** Design principles should evolve as user needs and business goals change. Be proactive in reviewing their relevance and advocating for changes if needed.

Understanding and applying guiding design principles is essential for any UX designer. These principles not only guide your daily work but also ensure that the products you help create serve the users effectively and align with the company's mission. As you progress in your career, you'll find that these principles are not just rules to follow but are foundational to designing exceptional user experiences.

07 Usability Heuristics

In User Experience (UX) design, the key to success lies not just in creating visually appealing interfaces but in ensuring they are intuitive and easy to use. Usability heuristics serve as guiding principles, leading designers through the maze of user interactions towards creating seamless experiences.

THE TEN USABILITY HEURISTICS

Usability heuristics, coined by Jakob Nielsen and Rolf Molich, are a set of broad principles that guide designers in evaluating the usability of interfaces. These heuristics are based on empirical studies and industry best practices, providing designers with a framework to identify and address usability issues effectively.

1. **Visibility of System Status:** Users should be informed of the system's current state and receive feedback on their actions promptly. Designers achieve this by incorporating visual cues such as loading indicators, progress bars, and status messages to keep users informed and engaged.
2. **Match Between System and the Real World:** Interfaces should speak the language of the users, employing familiar concepts and terminology. By aligning interface elements with users' mental models and real-world conventions, designers facilitate intuitive interactions and reduce cognitive load.

3. **User Control and Freedom:** Users should have the autonomy to navigate the interface effortlessly and recover from errors gracefully. Designers empower users by providing clear navigation paths, undo options, and intuitive exit points, ensuring a seamless and frustration-free experience.

4. **Consistency and Standards:** Consistency breeds familiarity, enhancing usability and learnability. Designers adhere to established design patterns, layout conventions, and interaction paradigms to create cohesive experiences that users can navigate with ease across different contexts.

5. **Error Prevention:** Prevention is better than cure when it comes to errors in UX design. Designers anticipate potential pitfalls and implement preventive measures such as validation checks, confirmation dialogs, and constraints to mitigate the risk of user errors before they occur.

6. **Recognition Rather than Recall:** Interfaces should guide users through tasks, minimizing the need for memorization and recall. Designers leverage visual cues, affordances, and contextual prompts to aid users in recognizing available options and actions, reducing cognitive effort and enhancing usability.

7. **Flexibility and Efficiency of Use:** Interfaces should cater to users with varying skill levels and usage patterns. Designers offer shortcuts, customization options, and advanced features to accommodate both novice and expert users, empowering them to accomplish tasks efficiently and with minimal friction.

8. **Aesthetic and Minimalist Design:** Beauty is not just skin deep; it influences usability profoundly. Designers strike a balance between aesthetics and functionality, employing minimalist design principles to declutter interfaces and prioritize content, thereby enhancing comprehension and engagement.

9. **Help Users Recognize, Diagnose, and Recover from Errors:** Errors are inevitable, but their impact can be mitigated through effective error handling mechanisms. Designers provide clear error messages, descriptive explanations, and actionable suggestions to guide users in diagnosing and resolving issues, fostering a sense of confidence and trust in the system.

10. **Help and Documentation:** While intuitive design is paramount, providing supplemental help and documentation can further enhance usability. Designers offer contextual help, tooltips, tutorials, and searchable documentation to support users in their journey, serving as a safety net for complex tasks and scenarios.

APPLYING USABILITY HEURISTICS IN PRACTICE

Understanding usability heuristics is just the first step; applying them effectively is where the real magic happens. Here are some practical tips for integrating usability heuristics into your design process:

1. **Conduct Heuristic Evaluations:** Regularly assess your designs against usability heuristics to identify strengths and weaknesses. Involve stakeholders, conduct heuristic evaluations, and prioritize actionable insights to drive iterative improvements.
2. **Iterate and Refine:** Design is an iterative process, and refinement is key to achieving optimal usability. Solicit feedback from users, conduct usability testing, and iterate based on real-world observations to fine-tune your designs and deliver exceptional user experiences.
3. **Educate and Advocate:** Usability heuristics are not just guidelines; they are principles to live by in the world of UX design. Educate your team, clients, and stakeholders on the importance of usability heuristics, and advocate for their integration into the design process to foster a user-centric mindset.

Usability heuristics are the North Star guiding designers by illuminating the path towards creating intuitive and delightful user experiences. By understanding and applying these heuristics in practice, designers can navigate the complexities of design challenges with confidence, ultimately paving the way to landing their dream job in UX design.

08 Design Language Systems (DLS)

In the fast-paced world of User Experience (UX) design, the ability to create consistent and scalable digital products is crucial. This is where Design Language Systems (DLS) come into play. A Design Language System is a comprehensive set of design standards and components that guide the creation of digital products. This chapter delves into what Design Language Systems are, why they are essential for UX designers, and how to effectively implement them in your projects.

WHAT IS A DESIGN LANGUAGE SYSTEM?

A Design Language System (DLS) is more than just a style guide or a set of UI components. It is a framework that combines the principles of design with the functionality of technology, ensuring a consistent user experience across all platforms and products. A DLS includes typography, color schemes, grid systems, spatial relationships, interactive elements and patterns, along with guidelines for their use.

A Design Language System is an invaluable tool for any UX designer looking to create harmonious, scalable, and efficient digital products. By establishing a clear and comprehensive DLS, designers can ensure that their work not only looks good but also feels cohesive and intuitive to users. As you embark on your journey in UX design, consider how a DLS can enhance your projects and help you achieve a more professional and consistent output.

1. **Consistency:** A DLS helps maintain visual and functional consistency across a product. This consistency is key to building user trust and understanding, as it provides a predictable and easy-to-navigate interface.
2. **Efficiency:** With a standardized set of components and guidelines, designers and developers can streamline their workflow. This systematization reduces the need for repetitive decisions and accelerates the design and development process.
3. **Scalabilitiy:** As organizations grow and evolve, their products must also adapt without losing their core identity. A DLS enables scalability, allowing for the expansion of product lines while maintaining brand coherence.
4. **Collaboration:** A well-documented DLS bridges the gap between designers, developers, and other stakeholders. It serves as a common language that everyone can refer to, simplifying communication and ensuring that everyone is aligned with the brand's objectives.

WHAT COMPRISES A DESIGN LANGUAGE SYSTEM?

- **Brand Identity:** The foundational understanding of the brand's mission, values, and target audience, guiding the visual and interactive elements of the system.
- **Design Principles:** Core principles that reflect the brand's identity, guiding design decisions and maintaining focus on user experience.
- **UI Components:** Reusable interface elements such as buttons, inputs, navigation features, and typographic styles, adaptable to various content and contexts.
- **Documented Guidelines:** Clear documentation on component usage, including instructions on layout, spacing, color usage, and interaction patterns, accessible to all team members.
- **Design Tools:** Software tools supporting the implementation of the system, managing design tokens, creating component libraries, and ensuring seamless updates across projects.
- **Education and Enforcement:** Training on system principles and components for team members, with regular project reviews to ensure compliance and updates to reflect new insights and technologies.

DESIGN LANGUAGE SYSTEM TEAMS

Design language teams are typically formed within organizations to manage and maintain design language systems (DLS). These teams are composed of multidisciplinary experts who collaborate to ensure consistency, coherence, and evolution of the design language across various products and platforms. Here's how such teams are typically formed and operate:

1. **Cross-functional Expertise:** Design language teams often comprise professionals with diverse skills and backgrounds, including designers, developers, content strategists, and product managers. This ensures a holistic approach to managing the DLS, considering both visual design and technical implementation aspects.

2. **Leadership and Ownership:** A designated leader or group of leaders oversee the design language team, providing strategic direction, setting goals, and ensuring alignment with the organization's objectives. These leaders take ownership of the DLS and champion its importance within the organization.

3. **Collaborative Culture:** Design language teams foster a culture of collaboration, encouraging open communication and knowledge sharing among team members. Regular meetings, workshops, and brainstorming sessions facilitate idea exchange and decision-making regarding DLS updates and improvements.

4. **User-Centric Approach:** The team prioritizes the needs and preferences of end-users when developing and refining the design language. User research, usability testing, and feedback collection mechanisms are integrated into the team's processes to inform DLS enhancements and iterations.

5. **Governance and Documentation:** Design language teams establish governance processes to maintain consistency and quality within the DLS. This includes creating and maintaining comprehensive documentation, style guides, and design principles that serve as reference materials for designers and developers across the organization.

6. **Tooling and Infrastructure:** The team selects and manages the tools and infrastructure necessary for creating, implementing, and maintaining the design language. This may involve utilizing design systems software, version control systems, and collaboration platforms to streamline workflows and facilitate cross-functional collaboration.

7. **Education and Training:** Design language teams invest in educating and training stakeholders across the organization about the DLS and its importance. Workshops, tutorials, and documentation are provided to empower designers, developers, and product managers to effectively utilize and contribute to the DLS.

8. **Continuous Improvement:** The team adopts an iterative approach to DLS management, continuously evaluating its effectiveness and seeking opportunities for improvement. Regular audits, performance metrics analysis, and user feedback loops inform ongoing refinements to the design language and associated processes.

By establishing and empowering design language teams, organizations can ensure the consistency, scalability, and usability of their products and services across various touchpoints, ultimately enhancing the overall user experience and brand perception.

09 Designing for Accessibility (A11y)

For aspiring UX designers, understanding and implementing accessibility is not just a niche skill—it's an essential aspect of your professional toolkit. As you prepare to enter the field of UX design, it's crucial to recognize that designing for accessibility widens your potential impact, enhances user satisfaction, and can differentiate you in the job market. This chapter will guide you through the fundamental principles of accessibility and explain why it is a critical component in creating effective and inclusive user experiences.

Understanding Accessibility

Accessibility in UX design means creating products that can be used by people of all abilities and disabilities. This includes a wide range of needs, from those pertaining to visual and hearing impairments to cognitive and motor skills disabilities. A well-designed accessible product ensures that all users can interact with it effectively, regardless of their physical or cognitive conditions.

The Four Principles of Accessible Design

The concept of accessible design is built around four guiding principles, often referred to as POUR, which make it easier for designers to remember and implement.

P.O.U.R. Framework for Accessible Design

1. **Perceivable:** Information and user interface components must be presentable to users in ways they can perceive. This could mean providing text alternatives for images, ensuring that audio content has a visual counterpart, or designing for various screen sizes and orientations.

2. **Operable:** User interface components and navigation must be operable by all users. Design for various interaction methods beyond traditional mouse and touchscreen inputs, like keyboard navigation, voice commands, and adaptive devices.

3. **Understandable:** The information and the operation of the user interface must be understandable. This means using clear and simple language, providing intuitive navigation, and helping users avoid and correct mistakes.

4. **Robust:** Content must be robust enough to be interpreted reliably by a wide variety of user agents, including assistive technologies. Ensure your designs are compatible across different devices and browsers and can adapt to evolving technologies.

The Importance of Designing for Accessibility

- **Enhanced Usability:** Designing with accessibility in mind generally leads to cleaner, more intuitive interfaces that improve the user experience for everyone, not just those with disabilities. Features that aid accessibility, such as high contrast visuals and logical navigation, enhance the overall usability of products.

- **Professional and Ethical Responsibility:** As a UX designer, you hold the responsibility to ensure that your designs are accessible. This commitment not only meets ethical standards but also complies with legal requirements, avoiding potential legal consequences.

- **Market Expansion:** Accessible designs reach a broader audience, including the millions of people with disabilities. This inclusion can significantly expand the market for a product and increase its commercial success.

- **Competitive Advantage in Job Market:** Demonstrating a strong competency in accessible design can set you apart in the job market. Employers are increasingly recognizing the importance of accessibility, and having this expertise can make your portfolio stand out.

Implementing Accessibility in Your Design Process

Start by incorporating accessibility into your design process from the outset. Use tools and guidelines like the Web Content Accessibility Guidelines (WCAG) as benchmarks. Regularly test your designs with a diverse range of users, including those who use assistive technologies. Stay updated with the latest developments in accessibility standards and technologies to ensure your skills remain relevant.

For those aspiring to make a mark in the field of UX design, mastering the principles of accessibility is indispensable. By embracing accessibility, you ensure that your designs cater to all users, reflecting both a high level of professional skill and a deep commitment to inclusive design. As you progress in your career, continue to advocate for and practice accessible design—it's not just good design; it's the right thing to do.

PART 2. UX Team Structures

10 UX Roles

There are several roles that work together throughout the product design lifecyle. Some companies combine roles into more of a "generalist" position; whereas some design teams have specialized roles. The following pages contain an overview of these roles.

UX DESIGNERS

UX Designers are the visual storytellers of the UX design ecosystem. They translate user needs into functional and aesthetically pleasing interfaces. Whereas some design teams have members in specialized roles and job titles, the UX Designer performs every aspect of design.

- **Information Architecture (IA) Development:** They define the organization of content and functionalities within the product for optimal usability.
- **User Flow Creation:** They map out user journeys, ensuring a smooth and intuitive flow for users to achieve their goals.
- **Interaction Design:** They create prototypes that illustrate the product's functionality and user interface.
- **Visual Design:** They apply design principles to create aesthetically pleasing user interfaces that are also user-friendly and consistent with the brand identity.
- **Accessibility Design:** They design with accessibility in mind, so products can be used by people with a wide range of abilities and assistive technologies.

UX RESEARCHERS

UX Researchers are the detectives of the UX design world. Their primary responsibility is to gather user data and translate it into actionable insights that inform design decisions.

- **Conduct User Research:** They employ various research methodologies like user interviews, surveys, and usability testing to understand user needs, behaviors, and pain points.
- **Analyze User Data:** They analyze user research data to identify patterns, trends, and key insights that inform the design process.
- **Create User Personas:** They synthesize research findings to develop detailed user personas that represent different user types with specific needs and goals.
- **Present Research Findings:** They effectively communicate research findings to the design team, stakeholders, and other project members.

VISUAL DESIGNERS

While UI/UX Designers often handle both user interface and visual design aspects, some organizations may have dedicated Visual Designers. These professionals focus on creating the aesthetic appeal of the product, ensuring it aligns with the brand identity and resonates with the target audience.

- **Visual Style Development:** Develop a consistent visual style guide that defines the product's visual language using elements like color palettes, typography, and imagery.
- **User Interface (UI) Design:** Work collaboratively with UX Designers to translate wireframes and prototypes into aesthetically pleasing and user-friendly interfaces.
- **Graphic Design:** Create graphics, icons, and other visual elements that enhance the user experience and brand identity.
- **Accessibility:** Ensure the visual design adheres to accessibility guidelines, making the product usable by people with disabilities.

CONTENT STRATEGISTS

Content Strategists focus on the words that users interact with within a product or digital experience.

- **Content Creation and Curation:** Develop compelling and informative content that aligns with user needs and the overall product vision.
- **Information Architecture:** Collaborate with UX Designers on defining the organization and hierarchy of content within the product.
- **Content Tone and Voice:** Establish the overall tone and voice of the user experience, ensuring consistency across all content.
- **Information Architecture (IA):** Work with UX Designers on defining the structure and hierarchy of content within the product for optimal usability and user navigation.
- **Accessibility:** Write content that is clear, concise, and easy to understand for users with different reading abilities or cognitive styles.

FRONT-END SOFTWARE DEVELOPERS

UI Developers translate the designs created by UI/UX designers into functional code. They are responsible for coding the user interface of the product, ensuring it works seamlessly across different platforms and devices.

- **Front-End Development:** They utilize programming languages like HTML, CSS, and JavaScript to build the user interface based on the design specifications.
- **Responsiveness and Optimization:** They ensure the user interface adapts and functions optimally across different devices (desktop, mobile, tablet).
- **Collaboration with UI/UX Designers:** They work closely with UX Designers to understand the design specifications and translate it into a functional product.

TEAM STRUCTURES

Organizations adopt different structures for their UX teams, each with its own advantages. UX design may be centralized as a shared service across product lines, or decentralized with dedicated design teams for each product line. When interviewing for a position, it's beneficial to inquire about the team's structure to understand its dynamics and how you might fit in.

- **Centralized UX Team:** A single UX team serves multiple projects or product lines within the organization. This structure helps maintain a consistent UX standard across all products.
- **Decentralized/Embedded UX Teams:** UX professionals are embedded within specific product teams, focusing solely on one product line. This structure allows deeper integration with product-specific issues but might result in varied UX standards across the organization.
- **Hybrid UX Team:** Combines elements of both centralized and decentralized structures. A central team sets company-wide UX standards and strategies, while embedded UX members tailor the user experience to specific products.

COLLABORATION WITH OTHER TEAMS

UX teams often work closely with other departments such as Engineering, Marketing, Customer Support, and Sales to ensure that the product meets both user and business needs effectively. This cross-functional collaboration is crucial for a holistic approach to product development.

The structure of UX teams is crucial as it impacts how effectively the organization can deliver user-centered designs and how quickly it can adapt to changing user needs or market conditions.

UX Team Collaboration and Alignment

1. **Partner with Leadership** — Partner with business leaders to understand Critical Success Factors (CSF) and Key Performance Indicators for the Business

2. **Partner with Product Managers** — Align UX work with short and long term business objectives to align and measure (NPS, CSAT, Cost to Serve, ASRt, Profitability and Sales)

3. **Partner with Business Analysts** — Partner with BAs to analyze requirements, identify the key needs (jobs to be done) and break down the work and deliverables

4. **Partner with Engineering** — Involve tech leads throughout the design phases to ensure technical feasibility and include their ideas and perspectives

5. **Partner with Stakeholders and SMEs** — User-centered Design includes customer and those who interface with customer (Sales, Services and Support) throughout the design process to ensure VOC (Voice of the Customer)

UX Process

UX Kickoff

Review business drivers with PM, BA, Technical Lead

Determine scope of UX process & timeline

Establish success criteria and timeline

Discover

Perform Research Sprint

Review Customer forums

Interview domain SMEs, Services, Support

Draw insights from usage analytics (Pendo)

Perform heuristic and competitive analysis

Ideate

Tailor ideation activities based on scope and business criticality

Conduct Design Sprint workshop (½ day to 5 days) although most prefer "lite"

Develop conceptual models and low fidelity (paper) prototypes

Prototype & Test

Create click-through prototypes in Axure, Invision or other

Perform iterative testing and refining with stakeholder involvement

Balance investment and time based on business criticality of solution

Specify & Deliver

Use prototype to socialize design

Tailor deliverables for business partners: BAs write JIRA stories, developers map design system components to code (redlines may be needed)

Perform UI Reviews during implementation

Measure feature success after delivery

11 UX Levels and Titles

The titles and levels within the UX Design field can vary across different organizations, but there is a generally recognized hierarchy that ranges from entry-level positions to senior leadership roles. This section provides an overview of common career levels from entry to senior level.

ENTRY LEVEL DESIGNER

- **UX Design Intern:** This is typically a learning and development role for individuals who are still in school or have just graduated.
- **Junior UX Designer:** Entry-level position for those with little to no professional UX design experience. They work under close supervision and are typically tasked with smaller, less complex aspects of the design process.

MID-LEVEL DESIGNER

- **UX Designer:** With a few years of experience, these designers handle more significant aspects of the UX design process. They work more independently and may start to lead smaller projects.

SENIOR-LEVEL DESIGNER

- **Senior UX Designer:** Possesses extensive experience and can manage complex projects. They often mentor junior designers and may have leadership responsibilities that include strategic decision-making.
- **Lead UX Designer:** Acts as the primary point of contact for UX design within the project or team, leading the design process and coordinating with other team members.
- **Principal UX Designer:** Holds a top-level individual contributor role, providing leadership and strategic guidance on major projects and initiatives, often across multiple teams or the entire organization.

MANAGEMENT

- **UX Manager:** Manages a team of UX designers. Responsible for the operational aspects of the UX team, including resource allocation, timelines, and project delivery.
- **UX Director:** Oversees multiple UX teams or the entire UX function within an organization. Sets the strategic direction for UX and ensures alignment with the organization's business goals.
- **VP of User Experience:** This executive spearheads the strategic direction and vision for user experience across all enterprise software products. They collaborate with key stakeholders to align UX initiatives with business objectives, ensuring a cohesive and intuitive user experience across the organization's software ecosystem.
- **Chief Experience Officer (CXO):** As the highest-ranking UX executive, the CXO oversees the entirety of user interactions with the company's software products. They lead efforts to unify user experience strategies, driving innovation and excellence in user-centered design principles across all platforms and touchpoints.

GENERAL NOTES

These titles not only represent increasing responsibility and skill but also an increasing influence on the strategic direction of product development and user experience.

- The progression through these levels depends on a variety of factors including education, individual skill level, and the specific demands and opportunities within each company.
- UX professionals often need to continuously learn and adapt to new tools, technologies, and methodologies to progress in their careers.
- Networking, a robust portfolio, and visibility in the UX community can also significantly impact career progression.

12 The Triad

While UX designers play a central role in crafting user experiences, they don't operate in isolation. The UX design ecosystem is a collaborative environment where various roles work together to ensure a successful customer experience.

THE TRIAD

In product experience design, the Triad approach involves Product Management, Design, and Engineering working closely together, similar to the three legs of a stool where each leg supports the structure. Product Management focuses on identifying the business problems that need solving. Design is responsible for determining the look and feel of the solution, ensuring it's both appealing and functional for users. Engineering ensures that what's designed can actually be built and will work as intended. This collaborative model ensures that from the start, a project is guided by clear objectives, practical design considerations, and technical feasibility, making it more likely to succeed in addressing both user needs and business goals.

Usually we think of it this way: "Product Managers define the requirements, Software Developers define the technology, and Designers define the form, behavior, look and feel."

The Product-Design-Engineering Triad

- Product – brings perspective on business viability
- Design – focuses on usability and delight
- Engineering – focus on feasibility and technology

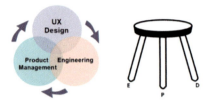

The triad model is a cornerstone of agile product development methodologies but is also applicable in various other development frameworks. Its fundamental value lies in fostering a balanced approach to product development, ensuring that the final product is desirable from a user and business perspective, viable from a financial standpoint, and feasible from a technical viewpoint.

1. **Product Management**
   - **Responsibilities:** Defines the product vision and strategy, prioritizes features, and sets the roadmap. Product managers (PMs) are the voice of the market inside the team, ensuring that the product aligns with business goals and customer needs.
   - **Focus:** Balancing user needs with business outcomes.
2. **UX Design**
   - **Responsibilities:** Focuses on how the product functions and feels from the user's perspective. Designers ensure the product is intuitive, effective, and satisfying to use. They handle user research, usability testing, interaction design, and visual design.
   - **Focus:** Advocating for the user's experience and needs.
3. **Engineering**
   - **Responsibilities:** Builds and implements the product according to specifications. Engineers ensure that the product works smoothly, meets performance standards, and remains maintainable and scalable.
   - **Focus:** Addressing technical feasibility and implementation.

IMPORTANCE OF COLLABORATION

1. **Ensures a Balanced Approach**

   By working closely together, the triad ensures that product development does not lean too heavily towards one aspect, neglecting others. For example, a focus purely on business needs without considering usability or technical constraints can lead to a product that is profitable but frustrating for users or impossible to build.

2. **Facilitates Communication**

   Regular interaction among the triad helps to quickly identify and address misunderstandings or misalignments across functions. This continuous communication ensures that everyone is on the same page, reducing the likelihood of costly revisions or pivots late in the development process.

3. **Encourages Innovation**

   When product managers, designers, and engineers collaborate from the start, they combine diverse perspectives that can lead to innovative solutions. This cross-functional creativity can result in unique features that are well-integrated, technically sound, and highly user-centric.

4. **Increases Efficiency and Reduces Waste**

   Close collaboration helps streamline the product development process, as decisions are made with a comprehensive understanding of constraints and opportunities from each domain. This can reduce cycles of revision, avoid feature creep, and prevent work on features that are not viable technically or valuable to users.

5. **Improves Product Quality and User Satisfaction**

   When all three perspectives are integrated into the development process, the resulting product is more likely to meet or exceed user expectations while fulfilling business objectives and maintaining technical integrity.

13 The UX Career Path

The typical career path for a UX Designer, starting from college to reaching the level of a Senior Product Designer, involves a combination of education, skill development, and progressively responsible professional experiences.

TYPICAL CAREER PATH

1. **Education**
   - **Bachelor's Degree:** Many UX designers start with a bachelor's degree in fields such as Graphic Design, Human Factors, Interaction Design, Industrial Design, Psychology, Human-Computer Interaction, or a related field. This provides a foundational understanding of design principles, user behavior, and technology.
   - **Courses and Certifications:** In addition to or in lieu of a degree, aspiring UX designers often take specialized courses in UX design, attend workshops, and obtain certifications to gain practical skills and a deeper understanding of user experience fundamentals.

2. **Entry-Level Positions**
   - **Internships:** Gaining practical experience through internships during or shortly after college is crucial. Internships provide hands-on experience and a chance to start building a professional network.

- **Junior UX Designer:** Starting as a junior UX designer or in a similar entry-level role, individuals typically work under supervision, handling smaller tasks such as creating wireframes, designing individual screens, and conducting basic user research.

3. **Building Experience**
   - **UX Designer:** After gaining some experience and proving their skills, UX designers take on more responsibilities. This can include leading smaller projects, engaging more with clients or stakeholders, and having a more significant role in the design process from research to prototype.
   - **Continuing Education:** Continuous learning is essential in UX design due to rapidly changing technologies and methodologies. UX designers often attend conferences, engage in new courses, and stay updated with industry trends.

4. **Mid-Level to Senior Roles**
   - **Senior UX Designer:** After several years of experience, a UX designer can move into a senior role. Senior UX designers handle complex projects, may lead multiple projects, and have more strategic input. They mentor junior designers and contribute significantly to design strategy and process improvements.
   - **Specialization:** Some designers choose to specialize in areas such as UX research, interaction design, or UI design, which can further enhance their career and value within teams.

5. **Leadership Positions**
   - **Lead or Principal Product Designer:** A Lead or Principal Product Designer typically has a broad role that encompasses UX, user interface (UI), and sometimes even product management elements. They focus on the overall product strategy, user experience, and design, ensuring coherence and effectiveness across all aspects of the product.
   - **UX Manager:** Experienced UX professionals may choose to go into management, where they lead design teams, oversee multiple projects, and have a substantial say in the strategic direction of projects or the organization's design approach.

- **UX Director:** UX Directors manage a team of UX professionals and oversee the UX strategy for multiple software products or the entire software suite. They collaborate closely with product managers and development teams to ensure that the user experience strategy is aligned with the goals defined for the business (known as Critical Success Factors, for further reading).

6. **Ongoing Professional Development**
   - **Networking and Community Involvement:** Engaging with the UX community through forums, groups, and professional networks like LinkedIn or local UX groups can provide opportunities for collaboration and professional growth.
   - **Portfolio Development:** Continuously updating and refining a personal portfolio is critical, as it showcases a designer's best work and evolution in their career.

The UX Designer's path is characterized by a continuous learning curve, hands-on project experience, and an increasing scope of influence in projects and within the organization. Each step builds on the previous one, providing more depth, expertise, and leadership opportunities.

PART 3. How To Get Started in UX Design

14 Essential UX Design Skills

So you're ready to embark on a career in UX design? This chapter dives into the core skills and knowledge you'll need to excel in this dynamic field. These skills can be categorized into the following areas: User Research, Design Thinking & Problem Solving, Design & Prototyping, UI/UX Specification, and UX Project Management.

USER RESEARCH SKILLS

Understanding user needs is the foundation of good UX design. Here are some crucial user research skills:

- **User Interviewing:** Conducting in-depth interviews with users to uncover their pain points, goals, and mental models.
- **Survey and Questionnaire Design:** Developing effective surveys and questionnaires to gather quantitative data from a broader user base.
- **Usability Testing:** Observing and analyzing user behavior while they interact with existing products or prototypes, identifying usability issues.
- **Data Analysis and Synthesis:** Effectively analyzing user research data to identify patterns, trends, and key insights to inform design decisions.
- **User Persona Development:** Creating detailed user personas that represent different user types with specific needs and behaviors.
- **Presentation of Findings:** Delivering key learnings to designers in an actionable format so they can inform ideation and solution development.

DESIGN THINKING & PROBLEM SOLVING SKILLS

UX design is all about solving problems with a focus on the user. Here are the key skills in this area:

- **Empathy:** The ability to understand and share the feelings of others. In UX design, this translates to putting yourself in the user's shoes and understanding their perspective.
- **Critical Thinking:** The ability to analyze information objectively, identify core problems, and develop creative solutions.
- **Ideation:** Generating a wide range of potential solutions through brainstorming and creative exploration techniques.
- **Prioritization:** Being able to prioritize design decisions and functionalities based on user needs and project constraints.
- **Decision Making:** Making informed design decisions based on user research data, usability testing results, and overall project goals.

DESIGN & PROTOTYPING SKILLS

UX design requires strong interaction design, visual design and prototyping skills to translate user needs into tangible solutions:

- **Information Architecture (IA) Design:** Understanding how to organize content and functionalities within a product for optimal usability and user navigation.
- **User Flow Creation:** Mapping out the steps users take to achieve their goals within the product, ensuring a smooth and intuitive user journey.
- **Wireframing and Prototyping:** Creating low-to-high-fidelity prototypes that illustrate the product's functionality and user interface. These prototypes are crucial for user testing and design iteration.
- **Design Principles:** Knowing and applying design principles like visual hierarchy, balance, white space, typography, and color theory to create aesthetically pleasing and user-friendly interfaces.
- **Basic Design Tools:** Having proficiency in design tools like Figma, Sketch, Adobe XD, or similar software used to create wireframes, mockups, and prototypes.

UI/UX SPECIFICATION & DELIVERY

Design plays a crucial role in specifying and delivering designs in a format that developers can easily implement. It's important to become familiar with these steps:

- **Finalize Designs:** The designer should have the ability to prepare final designs that are polished, with correctly named UI components that align with the company's software development kit. Spatial layout, color, font tokens, and responsiveness should comply with to the company's brand guidelines and Design Language System (DLS).

- **Prepare Deliverables:** The designer should know how to deliver designs in a format that can be consumed by developers. Some software programs include a dynamic inspector to observe front-end code, tokens, and components. Alternatively, some teams provide PDFs with manual annotations overlaid onto the views, indicating UI component names, layout details, font/color token details, interaction, and accessibility details.

- **Socialize Designs:** The designer should know how to organize a formal UI/UX Handoff meeting, especially for distributed teams, to orientate stakeholders and developers on how to access the UI/UX Specifications and interpret them. This meeting is also an opportunity to agree on where to link the specifications, and sets expectations for how the designer will support the team during the implementation phase.

- **Document in UX Repository:** A well-organized design team indexes design specifications in a centralized repository, along with supporting documentation for all phases of the lifecycle (research, prototypes, validation with users, and final delivery).

PROJECT MANAGEMENT

A large part of a UX Designers job is to manage many tasks throughout the lifecycle of design, from concept through delivery.

- **Agile Methodologies:** Applying Agile principles to manage projects, including Scrum, Kanban, and Lean UX.

- **Stakeholder Communication:** Effectively communicating with stakeholders to gather requirements and present design solutions.

- **Time Management:** Managing time effectively to meet project deadlines and deliverables.
- **Risk Management:** Identifying and mitigating risks throughout the project lifecycle to ensure successful delivery.

15 Learning Paths

The field of UX design welcomes individuals from diverse backgrounds. There's no single, one-size-fits-all approach to becoming a UX designer. This chapter will explore various learning paths you can consider to equip yourself with the skills and knowledge needed to launch your UX design career.

TRADITIONAL COLLEGE DEGREES

College degrees in design provide a comprehensive education in design principles, user experience, and human-computer interaction. Degree programs include Human Factors, Human-Computer Interaction, Interaction Design, User Experience Design, Graphic Design, and others. These programs offer foundational knowledge in visual communication, user research, and interaction design, complete with studio courses and a final project.

Benefits of Traditional College Degrees

- **Structured Learning Environment:** Formal programs provide a structured learning environment with a clear curriculum and dedicated faculty guidance.
- **Portfolio Building:** Degree programs often incorporate projects and assignments that can contribute to building a strong UX design portfolio.
- **Networking Opportunities:** Universities and colleges offer opportunities to connect with peers, professors, and industry professionals.

UX DESIGN BOOTCAMPS

These intensive programs offer a compressed and practical learning experience, often lasting from a few weeks to several months. They focus on equipping students with the core UX design skills and tools necessary to enter the job market quickly.

Benefits of UX Design Bootcamps

- **Practical Experience:** Bootcamps offer a faster and more affordable alternative to traditional degrees, often with a strong emphasis on practical skills and portfolio development.
- **Portfolio Material:** Be sure to choose a program that will help you walk out of the program with tangible UI/UX product design case studies that you can add to your portfolio and show in design interviews.

ONLINE COURSES AND SELF-DIRECTED LEARNING

A vast array of online courses and tutorials are available on platforms like Coursera, Udemy, Skillshare, and various universities offering online learning programs. These courses cover various UX design topics, from user research to prototyping. Numerous books, articles, and blogs offer valuable insights into UX design principles, methodologies, and best practices. With dedication and discipline, you can learn UX design through various self-directed learning methods, including online resources, attending industry events, and personal projects.

Benefits of Online Courses

- **Flexibility and Affordability:** This approach offers the most flexibility in terms of pace and cost, allowing you to learn at your own convenience and choose specific topics you're interested in.
- **Accessibility:** Online resources make UX design education accessible to a wider audience, regardless of location or financial constraints.

CHOOSING THE RIGHT PATH FOR YOU

The ideal learning path depends on your individual circumstances, learning style, budget, and career goals. Consider the following factors when making your decision:

- **Time Commitment:** How much time can you realistically dedicate to learning UX design?
- **Budget:** What financial resources can you invest in your education?
- **Learning Style:** Do you thrive in a structured environment or prefer a more flexible approach?
- **Specialty:** What specific area of UX design do you want to specialize in? (e.g., User Research, Interaction Design, Visual Design, Accessibility Design)

ADDITIONAL TIPS

Explore various learning paths, compare programs and online courses, and read reviews from past students.

- **Consider a Combination:** You don't have to limit yourself to a single approach. Combine online courses with self-directed learning or bootcamps to create a well-rounded learning experience.
- **Develop a Learning Plan:** Set clear goals and create a learning plan outlining what you want to achieve and the resources you'll use.
- **Get Involved in the UX Design Community:** Connect with other aspiring and experienced UX designers through online forums, meetups, or conferences. This can be a valuable source of knowledge, inspiration, and potential job opportunities.

No matter which learning path you choose, remember that UX design is a continuous learning journey. Stay curious, keep exploring new trends and tools, and actively seek opportunities to practice and refine your skills.

16 How to create a compelling UX Resume

In the competitive world of UX design, your resume and cover letter are your first chance to make an impression on potential employers. This chapter equips you with the tools to transform your resume and cover letter into persuasive documents that showcase your UX design skills and experiences relevant to the specific job you're applying for.

UNDERSTANDING WHAT EMPLOYERS LOOK FOR

UX design is unique in that it combines technical proficiency with creative vision and a deep understanding of user needs. Employers are looking for candidates who can demonstrate:

1. **Technical Skills:** Proficiency in one or more design tools such as Sketch, Adobe XD, Figma, and experience with prototyping tools like InVision and Axure.
2. **Problem Solving Abilities:** Evidence of how you've approached and solved user problems through design.
3. **User-Centric Approach:** Your ability to empathize with users and design solutions that meet their needs.
4. **Collaborative Spirit:** UX design is highly collaborative. Show how you've worked with other designers, developers, and stakeholders.
5. **Communication Skills:** Your ability to clearly articulate design decisions and their implications for the user experience.

STRUCTURE OF A UX RESUME

A compelling UX resume should be clear, concise, and well-organized, with a layout that itself reflects good design principles. Here's how you can structure your resume:

1. **Header:** Include your full name, professional title, and contact information. Optionally, add links to your LinkedIn, professional website, or portfolio.
2. **Professional Summary:** A brief section that summarizes your UX career, highlighting key skills and what you can bring to a team.
3. **Skills Section:** List your technical and soft skills. Use bullet points for easy reading and reference specific tools or methodologies.
4. **Professional Experience:**
   - Company Name, Location, Your Title, Dates of Employment: Start with the most recent.
   - Responsibilities and Achievements: Use bullet points to describe your responsibilities. Quantify achievements with metrics when possible, e.g., "Improved user session time by 20% through a redesigned navigation flow."
5. **Education:**
   - Your degree(s), the institution(s) you attended, and graduation year(s).
   - Any relevant coursework or projects.
6. **Projects/Portfolio:** Especially for newer designers, including key projects or case studies can be very effective. Briefly describe the project, your role, the outcomes, and the skills/tools used.
7. **Certifications and Awards:** Any relevant certifications or recognitions you've received.
8. **Professional Affiliations and Conferences:** Membership in professional organizations or participation in conferences.

THE ART OF THE TAILORED RESUME

Before diving in, research the company and the specific UX design role you're targeting. Understand their design philosophy, products and services, and the skills they value most. This knowledge becomes the foundation for tailoring your resume.

- **Highlight Relevant Skills:** Don't be a generalist. Analyze the job description and identify the specific UX design skills and tools they're seeking. Showcase your proficiency in those areas throughout your resume.
- **Quantify Your Achievements:** Numbers speak volumes. Whenever possible, quantify the impact of your design work. Did you increase user engagement by 15%? Reduce task completion time by 20%? Use metrics to demonstrate the value you bring.
- **Action Verbs are Your Ally:** Replace passive language with strong action verbs. Instead of "Responsible for user research," use "Conducted user interviews and surveys to identify user pain points." This demonstrates initiative and ownership.
- **Keywords: Your Resume's Secret Weapon:** Many companies use Applicant Tracking Systems (ATS) to screen resumes. Research popular UX design keywords and integrate them naturally into your resume content, but avoid keyword stuffing.
- **Readability is King:** Recruiters spend mere seconds scanning resumes. Maintain a clean and professional format with clear headings, consistent fonts, and ample white space. A one-page resume is ideal for entry-level positions, with a two-page maximum for experienced professionals.

TIPS

- **Proofread:** Typos and grammatical errors scream carelessness. Ensure your documents are meticulously proofread for any errors before submitting them. A single mistake can cost you the interview.
- **Design Consistency:** Maintain a consistent visual style across your resume and cover letter, particularly if submitting them electronically. Utilize a professional font, appropriate spacing, and subtle design elements to enhance readability.
- **Optimize for Online Applications:** Many companies use online application portals. Ensure your resume is formatted for easy upload and avoid using fancy fonts or graphics that might not translate correctly.

CRAFTING A COMPELLING COVER LETTER

- **Beyond the Resume Echo:** Your cover letter shouldn't simply echo your resume. It's your chance to tell a compelling story. Explain why you're applying to this specific company and this specific role. What excites you about the opportunity?
- **Personalize Your Introduction:** Always address your cover letter to a specific person, ideally the hiring manager. If the name is unavailable, use "Dear Hiring Manager" or "Dear [Department Name] Hiring Team." A generic salutation shows a lack of effort.
- **Highlight a Relevant Achievement:** Early on, showcase a relevant accomplishment from your past experience that demonstrates your design skills and problem-solving abilities. Briefly explain the challenge, your approach, and the positive outcome.
- **Align Your Values:** Connect your design philosophy and approach with the company's values and mission statement. This demonstrates a cultural fit and genuine interest in working for them.
- **The Call to Action:** Don't leave them hanging. Conclude with a call to action expressing your interest in an interview and providing your contact information for easy follow-up.

Remember, your resume and cover letter are a dynamic duo, working together to showcase your value as a UX designer. By tailoring them to each specific job application, you increase your chances of landing that coveted interview and launching your successful UX design career.

17 How to create a compelling UX Portfolio

For UX designers, a portfolio is not just a collection of work samples—it is a storytelling tool that showcases your skills, processes, and problem-solving abilities. It's often the first thing potential employers or clients look at, making it crucial for landing a job in UX design. This chapter will guide you through the process of creating a compelling UX portfolio that effectively communicates your expertise and individuality in the field.

THE PURPOSE OF A UX PORTFOLIO

A UX portfolio serves several key purposes:
1. **Demonstrates Your Skills:** It shows your ability to apply UX methods and design thinking to real-world problems.
2. **Showcases Your Process:** It provides insight into how you approach design challenges and iterate on solutions.
3. **Highlights Your Unique Perspective:** It reflects your personal design style and approach to user experience.
4. **Proves Your Professional Experience:** It offers tangible proof of your experience and capabilities in UX design.

It is important to understand that your portfolio is an ongoing project. Keep it updated with your latest work and adapt it to showcase your skills and experience as your career in UX design evolves.

COMPONENTS OF A UX PORTFOLIO

An effective UX portfolio should include the following elements:

1. **Introduction:** Start with a brief about yourself, your design philosophy, and what drives you as a UX designer.
2. **Case Studies:** These are the core of your portfolio. Each case study should cover a project from start to finish, including your process, solutions, and outcomes.
3. **Detailed Process Descriptions:**
   - **Problem Identification:** Explain the user problem you aimed to solve.
   - **Research:** Describe your research process, including methods and key findings.
   - **Ideation:** Show how you generated ideas and decided on a solution.
   - **Wireframes and Prototypes:** Include early sketches, wireframes, and interactive prototypes.
   - **User Testing and Feedback:** Discuss how user feedback was incorporated into your design.
   - **Final Solution and Impact:** Present the final design and discuss its impact, including any metrics that demonstrate its success.
4. **Visuals and Media:** Use high-quality images and videos to make your case studies engaging. Visuals should be accompanied by captions or short descriptions to contextualize them.
5. **Reflection and Learning:** For each project, reflect on what you learned and how you would approach the project differently in hindsight.

BUILDING YOUR PORTFOLIO

1. **Select the Right Projects:** Choose 3-5 projects that best represent your skills and range as a UX designer. Include a variety of projects that show your versatility.
2. **Tell a Story:** Each project should tell a story from the problem you were solving to the solution and its impact. Make sure the narrative is easy to follow and engaging.

3. **Focus on Your Role:** Clearly articulate your specific contributions to each project, especially if it was a team effort. This helps potential employers understand your capabilities and role preferences.
4. **Incorporate Testimonials:** If possible, include client or coworker testimonials that speak to your skills and contributions.

PORTFOLIO FORMATS

- **Online Portfolio Website:** This is the most common and flexible format. Platforms like Behance, Dribbble, or a self-hosted website allow you to showcase your work with visuals, descriptions, and interactive elements.
- **PDF Portfolio:** This format offers offline viewing and can be easily emailed to potential employers. However, it can be less interactive and engaging than an online portfolio.
- **Printed Portfolio:** While less common in the digital age, a well-designed printed portfolio can be useful for in-person interviews or industry events.

TIPS

- **Start Early and Continuously Update:** Don't wait until you have landed your first official UX design job. Start building your portfolio with personal projects, volunteer work, or freelance projects.
- **Tailor Your Portfolio to the Job:** When applying for a specific position, tailor your portfolio to highlight the skills and experience most relevant to the job requirements.
- **Get Feedback and Iterate:** Seek constructive feedback on your portfolio from other UX professionals, mentors, or design peers. Use this feedback to refine your portfolio and showcase your work effectively.
- **Showcase Your Process:** Don't just present the end results, offer insights into your design process. Include sketches, user flow diagrams and wireframes.
- **Storytelling:** Use your portfolio to tell a story. Capture the audience's attention by framing your projects as problem-solution narratives demonstrating your design thinking and problem-solving skills.

18 Acing the Design Interview

The resume and cover letter have opened the door, and now you've landed the UX design interview. This is your chance to showcase your design skills, problem-solving abilities, and most importantly, your passion for creating exceptional products and services. This chapter equips you with strategies and techniques to navigate the design interview with confidence and leave a lasting impression.

COMMON UX INTERVIEW DESIGN QUESTIONS

- **Tell Me About Yourself:** This is your chance to craft a compelling narrative. Briefly discuss your design journey, highlighting relevant skills and experiences. End by expressing your enthusiasm for UX design and why you're a perfect fit for the role.
- **Walk Me Through Your Portfolio:** Practice presenting your portfolio beforehand. Focus on projects most relevant to the job description. Explain your design process, challenges encountered, and the impact of your solutions. Remember, storytelling is key!
- **Describe Your Design Process:** Be prepared to articulate your UX design process from start to finish. Highlight your approach to user research, information architecture, prototyping, and user testing.
- **How Do You Stay Updated in UX Design?:** This question gauges your passion and dedication to the field. Discuss relevant resources you utilize, conferences you attend, or online communities you participate in to stay current on industry

- **Prepare for Behavioral Questions:** These questions explore your past behavior to predict future actions. Utilize the STAR method (Situation, Task, Action, Result) to structure your responses. Describe a situation where you faced a design challenge, the specific actions you took, and the positive outcome you achieved.
- **Design Challenges:** Many interviews will include a design challenge. This is your opportunity to showcase your problem-solving skills and design thinking in real-time. Ask clarifying questions, think aloud during the process, and demonstrate your ability to iterate based on feedback.
- **Technical Skills Assessment:** Be prepared for questions or tests assessing your proficiency in specific design tools like Figma, Sketch, or user research methodologies. Brush up on your skills beforehand and showcase your comfort level with these tools.

DEMONSTRATING PASSION AND COLLABORATION

- **Ask Insightful Questions:** Prepare a list of thoughtful questions for the interviewer. This demonstrates your genuine interest in the company, the role, and their design philosophy.
- **Express Enthusiasm:** Let your passion for UX design shine through! Convey your excitement about the opportunity and your eagerness to contribute to the team.
- **Highlight Collaboration Skills:** UX design is a collaborative process. Discuss past experiences where you worked effectively with developers, product managers, and other stakeholders.
- **Body Language Matters:** Maintain good posture, make eye contact, and project confidence through your body language. First impressions matter, and nonverbal communication speaks volumes.
- **Business Etiquette:** Follow up with a thank-you email after the interview. Express your gratitude for the opportunity and reiterate your interest in the position. This small gesture demonstrates your professionalism and leaves a positive final impression.

Remember, the UX design interview is a two-way street. While you're being evaluated, you're also evaluating the company and the role to determine if it aligns with your career goals and aspirations. Don't be afraid to ask questions and ensure the company culture is a good fit for you.

By following these strategies, practicing your responses, and demonstrating your passion for UX design, you'll be well-equipped to ace the UX design interview and land the job of your dreams.

19 Your First UX Design job

Congratulations! You've landed your first UX design job. This is a momentous occasion, marking the beginning of your journey in the field. However, transitioning into a new role can be daunting. This chapter equips you with strategies for navigating your first UX design position, adapting to a new work environment, and exceeding expectations to lay a solid foundation for your design career.

THRIVING IN YOUR FIRST UX DESIGN ROLE

- **Actively Learn and Be Open to Feedback:** Approach your first UX design job with a beginner's mindset. Be eager to learn from your colleagues, ask questions, and actively seek feedback on your work. Embrace constructive criticism as an opportunity to improve your skills and grow as a designer.
- **Become a Team Player:** UX design is a collaborative field. Build strong relationships with your colleagues, developers, product managers, and other stakeholders. Actively listen to their perspectives, communicate effectively, and work together to create exceptional user experiences.
- **Take Initiative and Demonstrate Ownership:** Don't be afraid to take initiative and suggest ideas. Proactively participate in discussions, identify potential roadblocks, and propose solutions. Demonstrate your ownership of projects and a willingness to go the extra mile.

- **Manage Your Time Effectively:** Prioritize tasks, set realistic deadlines, and learn to manage your time efficiently. There may be multiple projects on your plate, so effective time management is crucial for delivering high-quality work on time.
- **Document Your Process:** As you work on projects, document your design decisions, rationale, and user research findings. This will not only help you stay organized but also prove valuable for future reference and handoffs to other team members.

EXCEEDING EXPECTATIONS

- **Understand Your Company's Design Process:** Every company has its own unique design process. Take time to understand the specific workflows, tools, and methodologies used within your organization.
- **Deliver High-Quality Work:** Strive for excellence in everything you do. Pay close attention to detail, ensure your designs are polished and user-friendly, and always present your work in a professional manner.
- **Meet Deadlines Consistently:** Meeting deadlines is crucial for building trust and credibility. Develop a strong work ethic, manage your time effectively, and communicate any potential delays proactively to avoid setbacks.
- **Be Proactive in Learning New Skills:** The UX design field is constantly evolving. Take advantage of training opportunities offered by your company, attend industry events, and explore online resources to stay ahead of the curve and expand your skillset.
- **Become a Design Champion:** Be an advocate for UX design within your company. Educate colleagues from other departments about the value of UX design and its impact on the success of the business.

- **Build a Positive Reputation:** Maintain a positive and professional attitude. Be helpful to your colleagues, offer support when needed, and be someone others enjoy working with.
- **Find a Mentor:** Having a mentor can be invaluable for guidance and support during your first UX design role. Seek out a mentor within your company or network who can provide career advice and answer questions you may have.
- **Celebrate Your Achievements:** Take time to acknowledge your accomplishments, both big and small. Celebrate your wins and milestones to stay motivated and maintain a positive outlook.

Remember, embracing a growth mindset, actively learning, and exceeding expectations, you'll establish yourself as a valuable asset to your team and pave the way for exciting opportunities in the ever-evolving world of design.

20 Additional Information & Resources

To help you dive deeper into User Experience Design and strengthen your skills, here are additional resources.

BOOKS

The following books have been widely acclaimed within the UX design community and have contributed significantly to the field's understanding and practice.

- **"Don't Make Me Think: A Common Sense Approach to Web Usability"** by Steve Krug - This book is a classic in the field of UX design, offering practical advice on creating intuitive and user-friendly websites.
- **"The Design of Everyday Things"** by Don Norman - This book is highly influential in the UX field, exploring the principles of good design and how they apply to everyday objects and technology.
- **"Sprint: How to Solve Big Problems and Test New Ideas in Just Five Days"** by Jake Knapp, John Zeratsky, and Braden Kowitz - While not solely focused on UX design, this book introduces the concept of the design sprint, a time-constrained process for solving design problems and testing solutions quickly.
- **"Lean UX: Designing Great Products with Agile Teams"** by Jeff Gothelf and Josh Seiden - This book explores how UX design can be integrated into agile development processes, emphasizing collaboration, iteration, and a focus on delivering value to users.

ONLINE LEARNING COURSES

The following online learning platforms offer top-rated courses in User Experience Design.

1. **Interaction Design Foundation (IDF):** IDF offers a range of UX courses covering topics such as user research, interaction design, and usability testing. Their courses are self-paced and taught by industry experts. The platform emphasizes a strong theoretical foundation combined with practical application.

2. **Coursera:** This specialization offered by Coursera includes several courses covering user interface (UI) and UX design principles, prototyping, and user research.

3. **LinkedIn Learning (formerly Lynda.com):** LinkedIn Learning provides various UX design courses tailored to different skill levels and interests. Courses cover topics like UX research methods, wireframing, and information architecture, and they often feature industry professionals as instructors.

4. **Udemy:** Udemy hosts a wide range of UX design courses taught by instructors from diverse backgrounds. These courses cover various aspects of UX design, including user research, prototyping tools, and UX strategy.

5. **General Assembly:** General Assembly offers a full-time immersive course in UX design, along with part-time and online options. The curriculum covers UX research, prototyping, and user testing, providing hands-on experience through real-world projects. While it's a more comprehensive commitment, it offers an immersive learning experience with direct instructor support.

CONFERENCES AND WORKSHOPS

Conferences provide opportunities for UX designers to stay updated on industry trends, learn new skills, and connect with peers and thought leaders.

Some popular events for UX Designers include:

- **UX Design Week:** UX Design Week is a series of conferences held in different cities worldwide, offering a platform for UX professionals to learn from industry leaders, attend workshops, and network with peers. The event covers various aspects of UX design, including user research, interaction design, and usability testing.

- **UX London:** UX London is an annual conference held in London, UK, bringing together UX designers, researchers, and practitioners for three days of workshops, talks, and networking events. The conference features renowned speakers and covers topics such as design thinking, service design, and UX strategy.

- **UXPA International Conference:** Organized by the User Experience Professionals Association (UXPA), the UXPA International Conference is one of the largest gatherings of UX professionals globally. The conference features keynote presentations, workshops, and networking opportunities, covering a wide range of topics in UX design and research.

- **Config:** Config is an annual event organized by Figma, a popular web-based design and prototyping tool. It brings together designers, developers, and other creative professionals to explore the latest trends, best practices, and innovations in design and collaboration using Figma. Config features keynote presentations, workshops, panel discussions, and networking opportunities, providing attendees with valuable insights and inspiration for their design projects.

- **Adobe MAX:** Adobe MAX is Adobe's annual conference for creative professionals, including UX designers, graphic designers, and developers. While it covers various creative disciplines, the conference includes sessions and workshops specifically focused on UX design, showcasing Adobe's tools and featuring industry experts.

Glossary of UX Terms

The following terms are fundamental to understanding UX design and will serve as a helpful reference for topics of additional learning.

A/B Testing: A method of comparing two versions of a design to determine which one performs better.

Accessibility: Ensures usability of digital products for individuals of all abilities, fostering inclusivity.

Affinity Diagram: A visual tool used to organize and categorize ideas during a brainstorming session.

Affordance: Visual or sensory cues in a design that suggest how users can interact with an element.

Agile Development: A methodology for software development that emphasizes iterative development, collaboration, and customer feedback.

Business Strategy: A plan of action designed to achieve a specific goal or set of goals for a business, often involving market analysis, competitive strategy, and financial planning.

Card Sorting: A method used to help organize information logically, by allowing users to group items into categories.

Conversion Rate: The percentage of users who take a desired action, such as making a purchase or signing up.

Cognitive Load: The mental effort required to process information.

Customer Journey Map: A visualization of the process that a person goes through in order to accomplish a goal with your product or service.

A Critical Success Factor (CSF): Critical areas where performance must be excellent to ensure that objectives are achieved. They are often used as a way to measure the success or failure of a project or business strategy.

Design Thinking: A human-centered approach to innovation that involves understanding user needs, ideation, prototyping, and testing.

Design System: A collection of reusable components, guided by clear standards, that can be assembled together to build any number of applications.

Empathy Map: A visual representation of a user's attitudes, behaviors, and emotions regarding a specific problem or scenario.

Feedback Loop: A process where user feedback is used to make improvements to a product or service.

Fidelity: The level of detail and realism of a prototype or mock-up, ranging from low to high.

Fitt's Law: The time required to move to a target area is determined by the distance and size of the target.

Gestalt Principles: Describe how people perceive visual elements as a whole rather than individual parts.

Heatmap: Visually represents the frequency of user interactions with specific elements on a webpage.

Heuristic Evaluation: An assessment of a product's usability based on recognized design principles and guidelines.

Hick's Law: States the time taken to make a decision increases with the number of options presented.

Information Architecture (IA): Organization and structure of content to enhance user understanding and navigation.

Interaction Design (IxD): The design of interactive digital products and services, focusing on how users interact with them.

Key Performance Indicator (KPI): A measurable value that demonstrates how effectively a company is achieving key business objectives.

Lean Startup: An approach to developing businesses and products that aims to shorten product development cycles and quickly discover if a proposed business model is viable.

Market Research: The process of gathering information about potential customers, competitors, and market trends to inform business decisions.

Microcopy: Small, concise bits of text that guide users and provide clarity in the user interface.

Mobile-First Design: Prioritizes designing for mobile devices before considering larger screens.

Mockup: A model or replica of a machine or structure, used for instructional or experimental purposes.

MVP (Minimum Viable Product): The simplest version of a product that can be released to market to test its viability and gather feedback for future development.

Onboarding: The process of guiding users through initial interactions with a new product.

Progressive Disclosure: To simplify an interface, reveal information gradually to users to avoid overwhelming them.

Prototype: A simplified version of a product created to test and validate design ideas.

Responsive Design: Ensure seamless adaptability of products across devices, maintaining a consistent user experience.

ROI (Return on Investment): A measure used to evaluate the efficiency or profitability of an investment.

Stakeholder: An individual or group with an interest or concern in the outcome of a project.

Storyboarding: Illustrating a user's journey through a product using a series of images.

Token: In the context of a Design Language System (DLS), a token serves as a placeholder representing a specific design element, such as a color or font. Tokens ensure consistency in design across a system by allowing easy management and updating of design properties.

Usability: The measure of how easy or efficient it is for users to accomplish their goals using a product.

Usability Heuristics: The principles and guidelines used to evaluate the usability of a product.

Usability Testing: Observing users interacting with a product to assess its ease of use and identify improvements.

User-Centered Design (UCD): A design approach that involves users throughout the design process, prioritizing their needs and preferences.

User Experience (UX): The overall experience of a person using a product, including aspects such as usability, accessibility, and satisfaction.

User Flow: The sequence of steps a user takes to accomplish a task.

User Interface (UI): The visual elements of a product or system that users interact with, including screens, pages, buttons, and icons.

User Interface (UI) Design: The design of user interfaces for machines and software, such as computers, mobile devices, and other electronic devices.

User Persona: A fictional character created to represent the characteristics and behaviors of your users.

User Research: Gather insights into user behaviors, needs, and motivations to guide the design process.

User Satisfaction: The extent to which a user's needs, goals, and expectations are met when using a product or service.

User Journey: The path a user takes through a product or service, from initial contact to completion of a task.

Value Proposition: The unique benefit that a product or service offers to its customers, often expressed in a succinct statement.

Visual Hierarchy: Prioritizes content based on importance, guiding user attention and enhancing readability.

Whitespace: Empty space around design elements that enhances readability and clarity.

Wireframe: A basic layout to plan the structure and functionality of a webpage or app.

Wireframing: Creating a basic visual blueprint or skeleton of a webpage or app to plan layout and functionality.

N

Made in the USA
Monee, IL
02 January 2025

75862255R00071